I0606076

Travel in Space

Maria Koran

Go to **www.eyediscover.com** and enter this book's unique code.

BOOK CODE

AVE96473

EYEDISCOVER brings you optic readalongs that support active learning.

Published by AV² by Weigl
350 5th Avenue, 59th Floor New York, NY 10118
Website: www.eyediscover.com

Library of Congress Cataloging-in-Publication Data available on request

ISBN 978-1-7911-0774-1 (hardcover)

Printed in Guangzhou, China
1 2 3 4 5 6 7 8 9 0 23 22 21 20 19

072019
121818

Project Coordinator: John Willis
Designers: Mandy Christiansen and Sushant Deshpande

Weigl acknowledges Alamy, Getty Images, iStock, Newscom, and Shutterstock as the primary image suppliers for this title.

EYEDISCOVER provides enriched content, optimized for tablet use, that supplements and complements this book. EYEDISCOVER books strive to create inspired learning and engage young minds in a total learning experience.

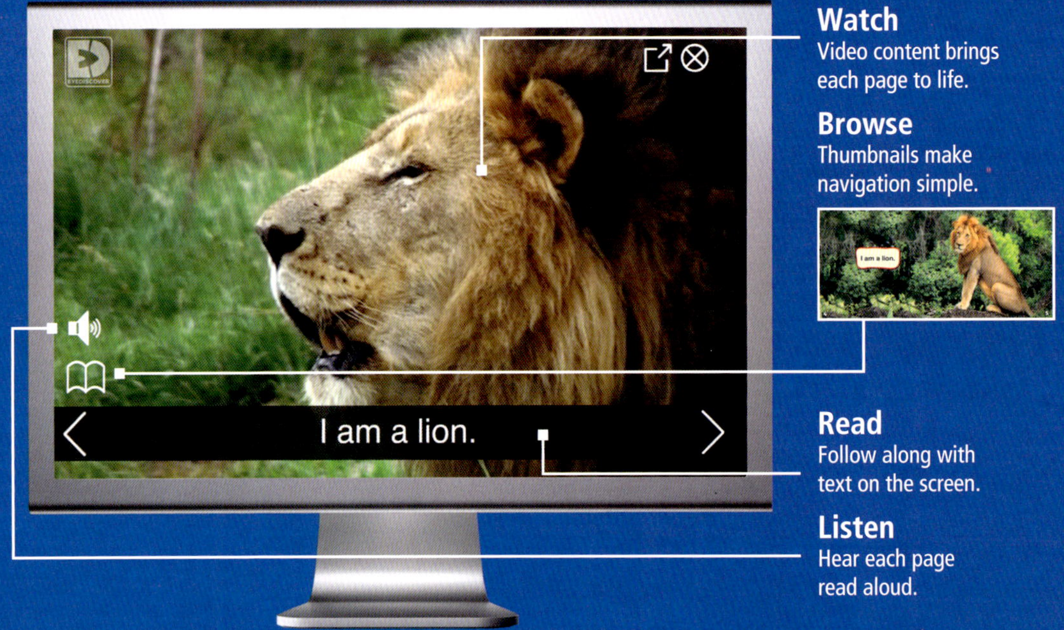

Watch
Video content brings each page to life.

Browse
Thumbnails make navigation simple.

Read
Follow along with text on the screen.

Listen
Hear each page read aloud.

Your EYEDISCOVER Optic Readalongs come alive with...

Audio
Listen to the entire book read aloud.

Video
High resolution videos turn each spread into an optic readalong.

OPTIMIZED FOR

- ✓ TABLETS
- ✓ WHITEBOARDS
- ✓ COMPUTERS
- ✓ AND MUCH MORE!

Travel in Space

In this book, you will learn about

- **how it began**
- **who does it**
- **how it works**

and much more!

Astronomers are people who study space. Early astronomers drew star charts to map the sky.

Galileo was an important astronomer. He made a powerful telescope more than 400 years ago.

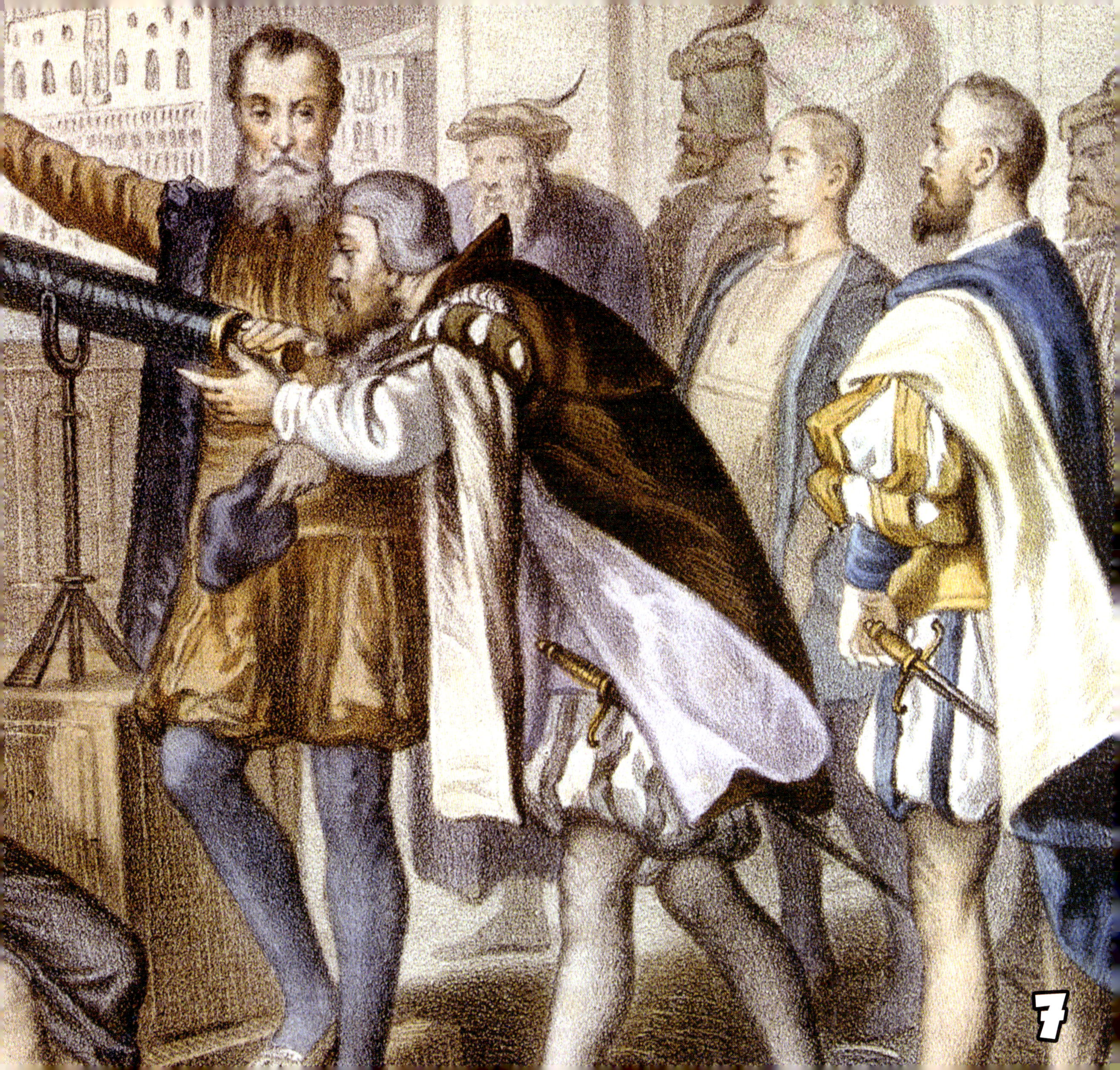

NASA

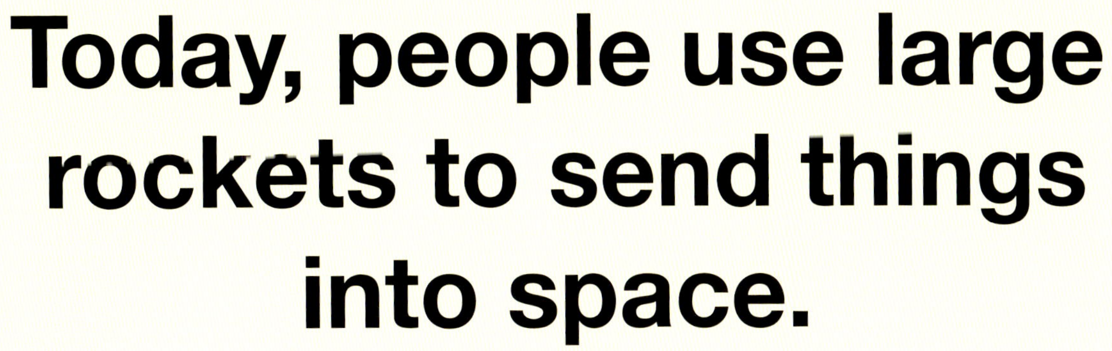

Today, people use large rockets to send things into space.

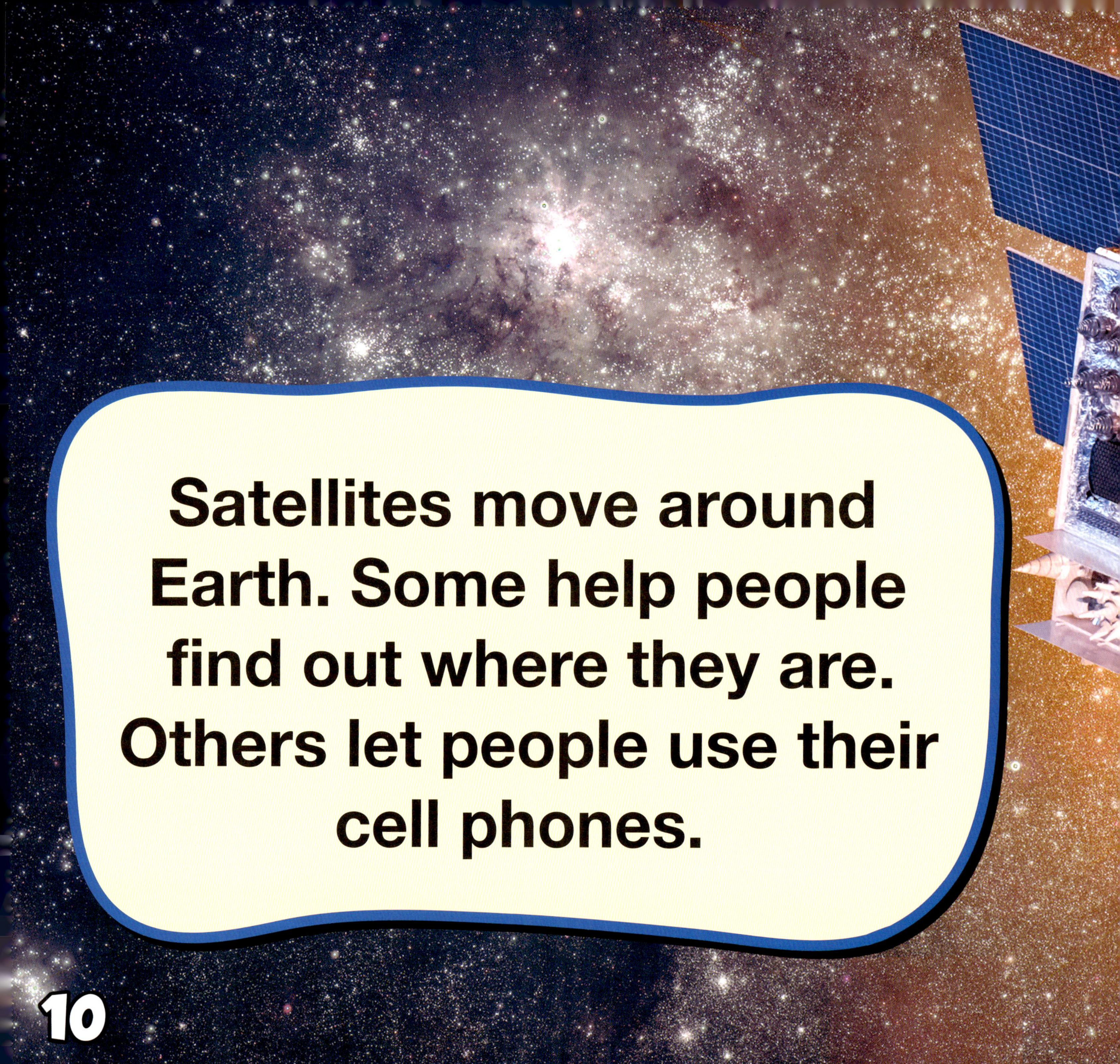

Satellites move around Earth. Some help people find out where they are. Others let people use their cell phones.

Yuri Gagarin was the first person in space. People who travel to space are called astronauts.

YAW
ELC
2·9

Astronauts wear space suits to keep safe. The suits give them air and stop them from getting too hot or cold.

Two U.S. astronauts landed on the Moon in 1969. Neil Armstrong was the first person to walk on the Moon.

Today, some astronauts work on the International Space Station. It was made by many countries working together.

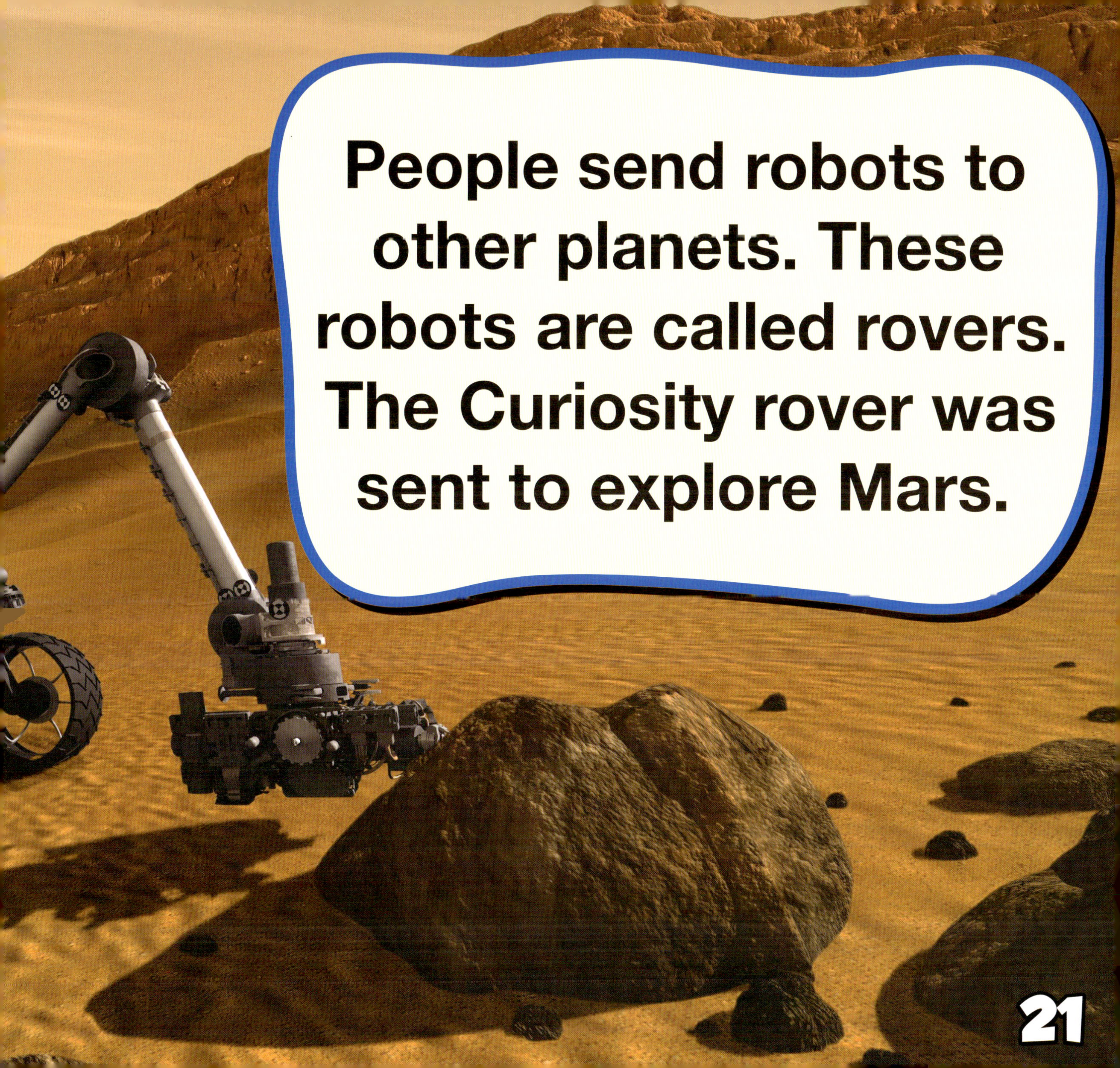

People send robots to other planets. These robots are called rovers. The Curiosity rover was sent to explore Mars.

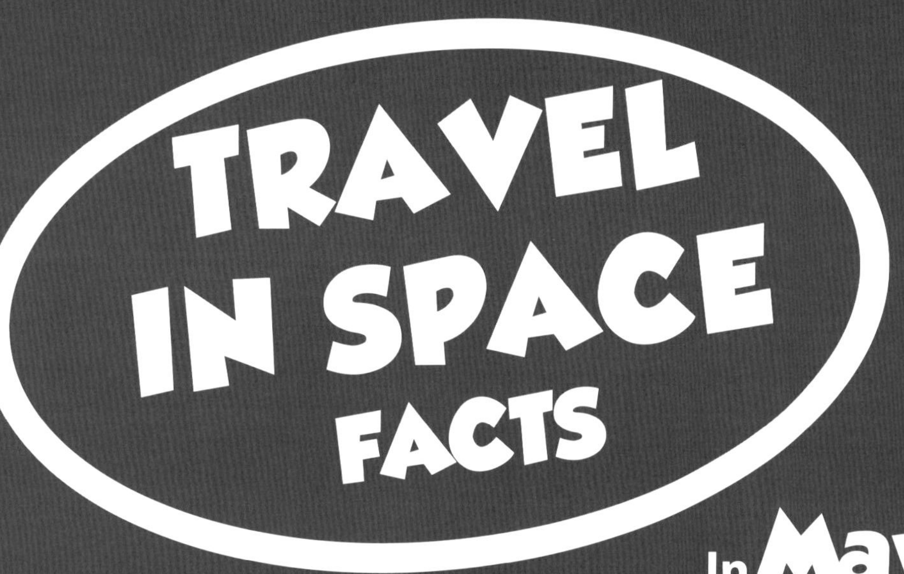

In **May 1969**, **John Young** became the first person to travel around the **Moon** alone.

Valentina Tereshkova is the **youngest** female **astronaut in history**. She was **26 years old** when she went to **space**.

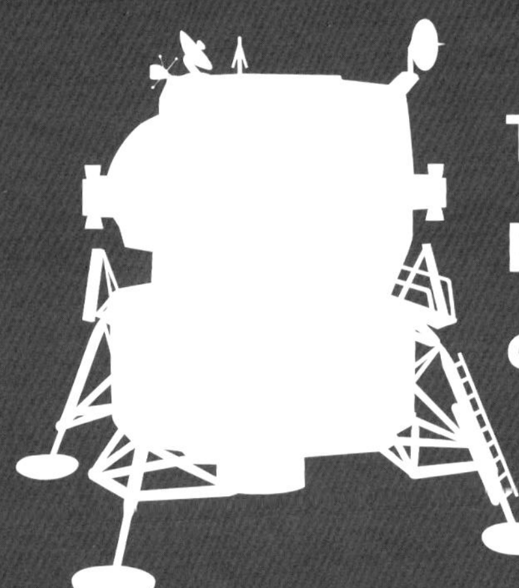

The spaceflight that first landed humans on the **Moon** was called **Apollo 11**.

When ***Neil Armstrong*** stepped on the **Moon**, he said ***"That's one small step for man, one giant leap for mankind."***

It would take about **9 months** for **astronauts** to travel to **MARS**.

KEY WORDS

Research has shown that as much as 65 percent of all written material published in English is made up of 300 words. These 300 words cannot be taught using pictures or learned by sounding them out. They must be recognized by sight. This book contains 50 common sight words to help young readers improve their reading fluency and comprehension. This book also teaches young readers several important content words, such as proper nouns. These words are paired with pictures to aid in learning and improve understanding.

Page	Sight Words First Appearance
5	are, people, study, the, to, who
6	a, an, he, important, made, more, than, was, years
9	into, large, things, use
10	around, Earth, find, help, let, move, others, out, some, their, they, where
12	first, in
15	air, and, from, give, keep, or, stop, them, too
17	on, two, walk
18	by, it, many, together, work

Page	Content Words First Appearance
5	astronomers, sky, space, star charts
6	Galileo, telescope
9	rockets
10	cell phones, satellites
12	astronauts, Yuri Gagarin
15	air, space suits
17	Moon, Neil Armstrong
18	countries, International Space Station
21	Curiosity rover, Mars, planets, robots

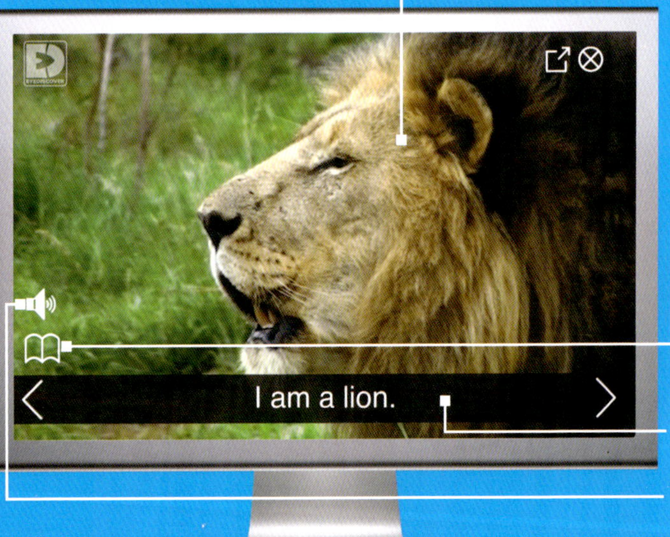

Watch
Video content brings each page to life.

Browse
Thumbnails make navigation simple.

Read
Follow along with text on the screen.

Listen
Hear each page read aloud.

Go to www.eyediscover.com and enter this book's unique code.

BOOK CODE

AVE96473